ECCENTRIC DICTIONARIES

#1

AN EXPERIMENT IN AI-ENHANCED HUMAN CREATIVITY

BY FREDERICK ZIMMERMAN

NIMBLE BOOKS LLC

Nimble Books LLC
2846 S. Knightsbridge Circle
Ann Arbor, MI, USA 48105

http://www.NimbleBooks.com

wfz@nimblebooks.com

Version 1.0; last saved 2021-01-13.

Printed in the United States of America

ISBN-13: 9781608882199

The paper used in this publication meets the minimum requirements of the American National Standard for Information Sciences—Permanence of Paper for Printed Library Materials, ANSI Z39.48-1992. The paper is acid-free and lignin-free.

DEDICATION

To human creativity.

CONTENTS

INTRODUCTION

I've always loved what I call "eccentric dictionaries." Under that heading I include both standard dictionaries with serious definitions that are salted with a hefty dose of personality, like Samuel Johnson's *A Dictionary of the English Language*, and humorous dictionaries with definitions not intended to be taken literally, like Ambrose Bierce's *A Devil's Dictionary*. It's been a long-standing ambition of mine to write and publish eccentric dictionaries of my own, but there wasn't an obvious way forward that didn't involve spending months tediously creating thousands of database entries one at a time—until I got my hands on OpenAI's GPT-3.

My goal was to create and publish a new eccentric dictionary in the spirit of Ambrose Bierce. I experimented with GPT-3's **davinci** and **instruct-davinci** engines until I was able to "engineer" (write) a prompt that reliably creates random dictionary entries in the style of Bierce. I wrote a script that ran the prompt repeatedly overnight and created a big text file of results. Then I began to edit and write.

It took me about two days to go from about 1000 randomly created entries to 641 that I liked, presented here as 114 pages in a 5 x 8" chapbook format. I discarded about 30% of the initial batch for redundancy or incomprehensibility (often due to my coding errors, not GPT-3's fault); I brought about 40% up to my standards with aggressive editing and writing; and about 30% required only light editing. A surprising portion of the total output—maybe 5-10%--struck me as brilliant and insightful. GPT-3 is an enjoyable collaborator that brings to the table a range of ideas and connections so wide as to be outside any individual human's scope.

Because the style exemplars by Bierce were written over a period from 1881 to 1911, the GPT-3 output contains some dated and potentially offensive concepts. I removed many but left some so as to retain the period flavor. Before proceeding further, readers should realize that not everything will be compatible with modern sensibilities. Where possible, I flagged problematic entries with comments like "Obsolete" or "Dated." I emphasize that responsibility for every word in this book is mine and mine alone.

GPT-3's generative capabilities include the capacity to create new words that have no actual equivalent in any known language. I noted these cases as "Neologisms". They are in fact sort of Super-Neologisms, more Neo than any ordinary neologism arising out of the normal processes of human language formation, and thus arguably even more interesting to word-lovers than regular neologisms.

GPT-3 also sometimes creates entirely plausible descriptions of facts that are not tethered to reality. Whenever there was a question in my mind as to whether what GPT-3 was saying was real, I checked a very well known search engine and added a note along the lines something along the lines of "Sadly, untrue".

As the subtitle of the book indicates, I consider this very much an experiment. I already have thought of ways to considerably improve the diversity and quality of future prompts, outputs, and final entries. In a world of continuous software delivery, the quality of algorithmically enhanced publishing should always be improving.

As the title of the book suggests, I see this as just the first in a series, and expect to publish additional *Eccentric Dictionaries* on a variety of topics as tech, popular culture, and politics. There will be batch templates for other types of books, too. I am working on a tool that will let third party authors request these batch templates and then submit their edited results to Nimble Books for publication.

GPT-3 is remarkable technology and there is a temptation to run the model and present the generated text output without editing as the evidence of "Artificial Intelligence." But as a lifelong book-lover, author, and publisher, my initial encounter with the technology has led me in the opposite direction. I may change my mind in the future as capabilities evolve, but for now, this is most exciting to me as a partner for enhancing *human* creativity.

Fred Zimmerman
Ann Arbor, Michigan, USA
31 December 2020

THE DICTIONARY

A, n. 1. The first letter and a vowel; a consonant when preceded by R. 2. The default grade at America's elite colleges (except Swarthmore).

AARDVARK, n. An arboreal, burrowing mammal of the order Tubulidentata, related to the elephant and lemur, living in Africa and India.

AARGH, n. 1. The sound made by a person who is frustrated because the device they are using appears to be broken. 2. The sound I made when I dropped my brand-new Samsung tablet on the bathroom floor and saw that I had cracked the screen.

ABIGAIL, n. Wife of Nabal (1 Sam. 25:2). Her name is given at the request of her husband's servants, to remind them that it was she who was then uppermost in his mind; but her continued usefulness resulted in her preservation for a life of domestic labor and thoughtfulness—the latter being an example of "emotional labor" 3000 years ago.

ABSENTMINDED, v. What you become after you graduate from college. See also: DEMOCRAT.

ABSTRACT, n. The essence of a conception, or the part which it retains when the concrete form expires.

ABUSE, v. To use unrighteous violence.

AGITATED, adj. Upset and nervous about potential calamities that may or may not be about to occur.

AGNOSTIC, n. One who denies the existence of knowable reality. See also: REPUBLICAN.

ALERT, adj. 1. Quick to perceive and act; showing quick wit or intelligent watchfulness; quick-witted. 2. Recognizing and responding to danger in encounters with enemies or wild animals. 3. An individual LERT.

ALL, adj. Containing everything within itself; whole, entire.

AMBITION, n. The desire of an individual to grasp opportunities to attain power not rightfully belonging to him.

AND, conj. A word rent asunder by a comma splice.

ANIMAL, n. A four-legged creature that has a soul, has the ability to think about its existence, and is conscious of the prospect of death.

ARGUMENT, n. A dialogue consisting in the main of unproven assertions advanced by one party and denied by the other.

ATTITUDE, n. A mental attitude in which the world is viewed as an unbroken expanse of grievance and misery; those having this attitude are broken-backed creatures.

B

BAH, interj. An exclamation of displeasure, disgust, or contempt. Normally followed by HUMBUG, a type of candy.

BEGGAR, n. One who possesses a natural gift for acquiring the property of others by the use of word or gesture. See also POLITICIAN.

BELIEF, n. An intellectual crime. Incorrect beliefs are subject to sentence without mitigation.

BEZOS, JEFF. An amiable man of vast wealth, who is the living proof of Darwin's theory that survival depends on being at least as stupid as your competitors.

BLASPHEMY, n. Words uttered against God, the Lord Jesus Christ, or the Holy Ghost, imputing to them matters unworthy of Their high office, or accusing Them of deeds inconsistent with Their goodness and justice and holiness; such as are blasphemy against the Holy Ghost, saying that He blasphemeth. See also: WOKEISM.

BLONDES, n. Plural of "blonde."

BOLLOCKS, pl. of Bollix. Multiple exclamations of nonsense, as uttered by those who deny the gods; or by a babeswho would force his mother to bear his sins; or by a destroyer of systems of religion and ethics, who knows nothing about them.

BREAKFAST, n. The first meal; also the last supper. Jesus spent

BRIGHT, adj. Intelligent, enlightened. At most 20% of the population. This is a problem.

BULLY, n. One who has a superficial appearance of strength and power but without the intellectual capacity to properly apply it. See: TRUMP, DONALD.

C

CALAMITY, n. An event that is not to be desired. See also: 2020.

CATASTROPHE, n. A convenient word for describing violent upheaval or destruction. See also: 2020.

CHARACTER, n. A personification of consistency between motive and action. "His life is a narrative of the truth that consistency is the hobgoblin of little minds, only adored by little statesmen, philosophers and divines. In life as well as in fiction he has been the invariable protagonist of every piece, with truth for his antagonist." See: TRUMP, DONALD.

CLEAN-MINDED, adj. Being in a state of mental and moral excellence from which unclean thoughts flow as from a rancid butter tub with false bottom.

CLICHE, n. A trite or tiresome remark—one that is repeated indiscriminately ad infinitum by today's technologies.

COMMANDER, n. See BOSS; SPOUSE.

COMMITTEE, n. A group of people who can do nothing individually and sit around a table to decide that nothing can be done together.

CONFEDERATES: Many wonder why we still persist in calling them Americans. The death Stonewall Jackson was a great defeat for believers in "The Lost Cause", and that is sad. But the ache of an old wound is nothing to the pain of the new ones that racism inflicts every day. This must change. As Thucydides says, "The strong do what they may; the weak suffer what they must." It is now the Confederates who are weak.

CONQUEROR, n. One who does what others cannot do. Example: "Kang the Conqueror will defeat the Avengers."

CONSCIENCE, n. 1.A still small voice within a man's breast that warns him that he proposes to do something dishonest, inconsistent, unwise. 2. That which warns us we are about to do wrong; the power of distinguishing right from wrong in order to decide which is the better or expedient. 3. The inner voice which warns us that someone might be looking. Distinguish from: REPUBLICAN.

CREED, n. A statement of our beliefs which nobody else can understand but which we find plausible and consoling.

CURDLEDY-TIMBERS, n. Creepy but fortunately nonexistent spiders who spin silken rings covered with poison, fatal if you accidentally ingest a web. Neologism.

CURIOUS, adj. Singularly pertinacious in questioning one's patience and self-control. A severe trial to both these qualities.

DEAREST, adj. Most probable agent of human unrest and disturbance.

DECADE, n. In the sequence of decades, a period of ten years, ending with a zero—or time spent on Zoom meetings in 2020.

DECENT, adj. Fitting; suitable; agreeable; comely. Obsolete.

DECIDE, v. To settle a question or a matter as to which there are two or more different solutions or courses of action.

DEMOCRAT, n. A member of a political party who is not a Republican. Admitting that the party has been seen as "elitist," they are trying to rebrand themselves as "cool" and "progressive." They are currently doing this by throwing Democratic National Committee fundraisers in Brooklyn featuring such cultural icons as David Byrne, Moby, and St. Vincent. On track until we hit David Byrne.

DESIRE, n.: That which tyrannises us.

DEVIL, n. An angel who sinned.

DISAGREEMENT, n. A point on which persons who cannot both be right must disagree.

DISCRETION, n. A particular kind of ignorance, briefly characterized as forgetfulness when convenient.

DISTINGUISHED, adj. Separated from others in respect to rank, eminence, or any other quality, however arbitrary or artificial.

DISTURBER, n. One who by his example or profession tends to make things uncertain. See SCIENTIST.

DOCTOR, n. 1. A healer of souls and bodies. 2. (honorific) Jill Biden and every other person who has ever received a doctorate will now be referred to by this honorific.

DOGMA, n: Of no value unless it can be interpreted. "The dogma is strong within her."—Senator Dianne Feinstein, referring to the Catholic Supreme Court nominee Amy Coney Barrett.

DRAGON VEIN OPIUM: A tonic to ease constipation. This does not seem to really exist, but it would be awesome if it did, and one hell of a lot better tasting than Miralax™.

DRIFT, n. The general direction in which people are going; the current of opinion and feeling in a certain direction.

E

ELLIPTIC, n.: A French word of Greek origin, meaning "loose thread." Untrue, but the relationship between loose thread and the Furies would give new meaning to the term "ellipitical threat."

ELON MUSK, n. Prominent astralnaut, explorer of the cosmos and collector of rare works of art: his crowning success: The Falcon Heavy.

ELON MUSK: A legendary anti-corruption officer. Sends virgins to the old men.

ENJOY, v. To obtain from another's discomfort the sensation of a complacent smile.

EQUALITY, n. A condition or relation of momentarily equal standing.

EQUALITY, n. In law a word meaning that those named in the equality shall be treated alike, but with an inevitable result that they will each receive something different.

EUROPEAN UNION: Absinthe and gendarmes. This union has a mind of its own, situated in Berlin.

EVANGELIST. A priest of one of the Christian faiths, as distinguished from the Papal self-deception, from the Hindoo confidence trick, or from Islam.

EXCUSE MY BLUE! Steve Martin, cursing.

F

FALSEHOOD, n. An abominable act that is next to serving one's country as an unpardonable crime against patriotism and all mankind.

FAMOUS, adj. Conspicuously miserable.

FARCE, n. Fustian text of straw charmingly appropriate to a foul purpose.

FEMALE, n. One of the two sexes distinguished from the other by various physical and functional characteristics such as XX chromosomes and a uterus that can gestate human offspring.

FORKED RIVER WAR: A conspiracy attributed to Tim Hortons between the time they opened a shop in Toledo and two weeks later when a Tim Hortons franchise was put in Detroit. Ohio and Michigan are still at war. Doubtful veracity.

FRIEND, n. 1. A person whom one knows and likes. 2. One inclined to sympathize more with our sorrows than with our joys.

FRIENDSHIP, n. A word invented by poor or lowly people to signify a conciliatory love for those who have a little property and prestige.

G

GENIUS, n. A vernal and fructuous power that fertilizes the human mind.

GENTLEMAN, n. According to J.K. Rowling, a man who is one of the two sexes distinguished from the other by various physical and functional characteristics such as XX chromosomes and a penis that can penetrate a woman's vagina.

GESTICULATION, n. The act of miming the point of impact to another part of a body, as in aiming from the hip or touching a finger to with side of nose.

GOOD-BYE, int. A parting salutation to one going on a journey or on an errand. By it we express our hope that he will have a pleasant journey or a good success attending him above all hazard; as also assurance of our esteem for his character, let what may betide.

GOOD, adj. Used to refer to a variety of subjects; including an action or situation that benefits someone else in addition to oneself, or which has no harmful consequences for anyone involved; any unbroken object that is not a machine; something that is enjoyable or pleasing. "Positive sum."

GOUT, n. In France, slander and libel are no longer prosecuted. Gout is.

GRAMMAR, n. The art of demonstrating one's knowledge of arbitrary rules about the arrangement of words to disguise the fact that any rational sense they may possess had been left out long ago. See also: GENERATIVE TEXT GENERATION.

GREEDINESS, n. An excessive desire to take everything for oneself and not share with others, especially desirable resources or power.

GREEKS: Always whinging about Turkey and the Elgin Marbles.

GUILLOTINED: The Hamlet of France: a soliloquoy cut short.

GUILT, n. 1. The state of one who has committed an offense. 2. The feeling arising from consciousness of having committed such an offense. 3. In modern popular culture, guilt is established by the testimony of the online mob; the tribunal which pronounces the judgment of "guilty" is composed of such persons as believe that may have been wronged by the criminal, or whose need to express their feelings controls them; the prosecutors are those people whose site traffic will decline if they are boring; and the only defense attorneys are masochistic contrarians. During the trial, any person can volunteer information without vetting, and no witnesses shall be stricken from the list unless their evidence contradicts the dominant media narrative.

HEARSAY, n. That which is excluded from evidence because of its obvious relevance.

HEAT, n. The rate at which energy is transferred from one body to another through contact without the exchange of sensible heat; what makes things hot. See GREENHOUSE EFFECT.

HEAVENLY BLUE GAS: Poetry. No offense to my daughter, who is a poet.

HELP, n. The kind of assistance that is most needed by those who have the least ability to give it.

HEPBURN, n. The part of a garment that covers the neck.

HISTORY, n. 1. A fanciful narrative of events, mostly false, which are either not important or did not happen at all. Example: the traditional self-congratulatory narrative of American exceptionalism. 2. 2. A thematic narrative composed of events completely tragic, carried out exclusively by evil people from the past, and requiring the highest priority in the present day.

HOLLAND, n. Seven provinces and a bunch of people speaking Flemish.

HOME, n. The most common American rural dwelling-house, in its vernacular acceptation. Formerly, a small brown house usually perched on a brick or stone foundation. Now, an outer-ring post-housing crisis McMansion.

HOMEOPATHY: Recovery without pills. It would have to be, since homeopathic doses have no effect.

HORSE RACE, n. The sport of kings. A contest in which the noble four-footed participants run over a little ground while a great crowd stands around and watches them.

HUMANITY, n. The human race collectively, viewed as asses with a pedigree and a fancy Latin name.

HYPERLOOP, n. A proposed underground transportation system using individual cars carrying single people or small groups at speeds slower than trains carry hundreds.

I

INDIAN, n. A person whose skin has a reddish hue. The generic name for the red men of America, in North and South and Central America, and in the Islands of the Carib sea; applied to them collectively, or to any member of their tribes. Obsolete.

INDUSTRY, n. A particular kind of legally sanctioned villainy chosen over more violent alternatives merely because it is more profitable than them.

INERTIA: The tendency of the dead to remain in the living.

ISLAND, n. A piece of land entirely surrounded by water. The most famous English example is the Isle of Wight.

J

JAPANESE: They make Godzilla and robots. And drink absinthe only in secret.

JOURNALIST, n. the last person to be trusted with real information.

JUSTICE, n. A commodity in an adulterated condition. The market price is increasing daily, although the product is not visible.

KILL, v. To create another's death by power that resides in oneself or at one's command.

KNIFE, n. An instrument used chiefly for the purpose of cutting nothing.

KNIGHT, n. 1. A man who lives by the labor of his hands and of his mind, as opposed to a gentleman, who does it mostly by borrowing. 2. A mounted soldier armed with a long sword, whose object in time of peace is to knock down some other soldier who is also mounted and armed with a long sword.In time of war he kills various enemies unmounted and unarmed.

LIBERAL, adj. Pretending to love everything but practiced at loving nothing but one's — self.

LOCATION, n. A geographical place used for determining your value as an advertising product.

LOGOLITHONOMY: The science of beautiful words. Neologism, apparently derived from the resemblance of beautiful words to gems.

LOVE, n. 1. The ultimate exaggerator of the distances of separation. 2. A temporary insanity curable by marriage. 3. An emotion that is made of a single soul inhabiting two bodies and inspired by two distinct pleasures and two divergent ideas. 4. An emotion with which Nature compensates the human being for what she withheld in the matter of brains. 5. To have both the deep appetite and the intellectual apprehension required to behave with complete selfishness.

LOW VOICE: The essence of the low feelings and drunken brains evoked in conversation with Amazon's Alexa "whisper mode."

MAGA, n. A word that has lost its meaning.

MAN, n. A biped who is occasionally rational and sometimes wears clothes. Obsolete. Person is now preferred.

MANDARIN: A pig-headed, stuffy pot from Peking. In Blade Runner 2049 future will be used to welcome LA's new Chinese overlords.

MANIA, n. An unreasonable and excessive enthusiasm; a craze for something.

MARRIAGE, n. The state or condition of being united to a person for life.

MATHEMATICS, n. Known as the science of numbers; because numbers are the only things that never change in any way whatever; as the science of quantities, because they are the only things that can be counted with accuracy; as the science of order, because they are less likely to change their position than anything else in our world; and as the science of relations, because they show us what relation one thing has to another, while all other sciences tell us what it is something like. It's no wonder many people are afraid of mathematics.

MATTER OF FACT, adj., adv., n., v., etc. When we talk about "matters of fact" we are referring to "opinion" as opposed to "fact."

ME: You hadn't noticed?

MEDIA n. In its broadest sense, a device for obscuring the distinction between command and choice.

MEDICINES, n. Substances which, variously, open the pores of the skin, correct eruptions on the surface which then close and heal without leaving a scar, stopscertain troubling thoughts in the mind, alleviate certain unpleasant emotions in the soul, bring some relief to sick creatures and, after convalescence, enable the recovered to do their work more adequately.

MERCY, n. The human attribute that links us all to the divine. The belief that MERCY literally means "womb-cord" appears to be profoundly untrue, but it is not without psychological truth.

MILITARY, n. The profession of arms in its two great branches of service: strategy and tactics.

MONASTERY, n. In modern cities, a tall building with a steel-framed and concrete shell, with the sides sheathed in impermeable glass windows to keep out the grave menace of air circulation, that might produce healthy workers who are not tethered to their desks.

NAPOLEONIC, adj. That quality of male ego which requires a woman whose manner proclaims "I am a woman adorned with jewels and laziness."

NASING, adj. Offering an insincere compliment meant only as innuendo to attribute dishonour by invoking another's good qualities. "If you repent, and desire to be forgiven of sin—why, pray abandon your appeal." Neologism. No evidence can be found that this is a real word, but if it existed, it would be a good one.

NESSIE, n. A serpent with the body of a worm and the head of a rabbit.

NIGHT, n. The appointed and sadly limited time for rest from toil and wickedness, till morning restores what evening has robbed, the opportunity to sin again.

NON-CONFORMIST, n. A person whose life is an anti-pattern.

OATH, n. The formal declaration taken to justify the truth of what is uttered by the swearer, in a court of law or elsewhere. Great weight is placed on keeping oaths taken in legal settings despite our society placing almost no weight on oaths taken elsewhere.

OUT-TROPHE, v. Mental ability: a capacity for quickly forming a new idea or concept, and administering it to others so that they, too, can use it. A first-rate naval architect may be outrouphal in mathematics and physics. A first-rate HISTACTERIST may be outrouphal in facts and psychology. "To be outrouphal means you have large powers of overcoming obstacle, for you are abouot to make others more capable." Neologism.

OUTTABS, n. Climbing equipment generally worn under clothing: the holsters are called "outslots". Worn by men who may need to climb trees at a moment's notice, or by firemen at home if they must do something more than get up from bed.

OWN THE OLD LAW, n. To refuse the laws of a past administration, and instead of fulfilling them, maintain by force these principles on which your national welfare is founded. Example: "Had Trump won in 2020, a Democratic administration elected in 2024 might have had to 'own the old law' to restore Constitutional government despite the superfically legal rulings of the Republican Congress and Supreme Court." Neologism.

P

PAGE JONES, n. A passionate love for reading.

PARADISE, n. The Garden of Allah in the current limited sense of the word confined to Far Western Asia (otherwise known as Europe). It is so called in jest because most of Far Western Asia has been appropriated by Christians. Untrue.

PASTIME, n. A deliberate effort to forget the boredom which one suffers in the present.

PATHOS, n. The quality in discourse or writing which provokes tears. Different emotional states are classified under this head, as the pathetic (sorrowful), the oleaginous (timid), the ironical (objecting), the severe (stern), etc.

PATRIOTISM, n. Combustible rubbish ready to the torch of any one ambitious to illuminate his name. See MAGA.

PEACE, n. In international affairs, a period of cheating between two periods of fighting. Unsatisfactory condition that comes in the wake of a war.

PEOPLE, n. A multitude of men, women, and children whose chief occupation is to amuse one another.

PHILOSOPHY, n. A route of many roads leading from nowhere to nothing.

PIER, n. An obstruction in the water near the shore, making it difficult to Jet-Ski directly along the beach.

PISSY PREAMBLE, n. An ungentlemanly prefatory fragment prefixed to an address to any person, often of a broadcast naturer and not merely to the nominal audience..

PLAQUE POISONER (GLITTERING BUDDY), n. That evil toothpaste containing fluoride that you use. Cares little for you if you are ugly, only works for people who already have beautiful teeth, Vulgarism used only by ignorant anti-vaxxers. Neologism.

PLATE, n. A broad, round piece of metal. Supposed to be a dish.

POETRY, n. 1. The art of employing words so as to give an appearance of sense to expressions that have no meaning. 2. The art of misapplying words for humorous and sentimental purposes.

POLICE, n. The uniformed arm of the law usually prefixed with "gendarmerie."

POLITICAL PARTY, n. A group of citizens with delusions that they're somehow controlling things. These delusions are sometimes exposed during primary elections, as in 2016.

POLITICIAN, n. 1. One engaged in the noble and useful profession of securing money votes from a densely ignorant electorate by promising to protect it from its own best interests. 2.. An eel in the fundamental mud upon which the superstructure of organized society is reared. Whenever he wriggles, he belches the slime upon which he rests.

POLITICS, n. A strife of interests masquerading as a contest of principles. The conduct of public affairs for private advantage.

POLYSYNAPTIC DEVIL-MINDEDNESS, v. To stretch one's attention beyond natural interest and capacity to a great variety of topics. Me.

POSITIVE ATTRACTION, n. A love that breeds, rather than kills, rabbits.

POST, n. A support consisting of an upright beam supporting another, especially when designed to be set into the ground. By extension, a building or a part of a building erected on this support.

POST, v. To erect (a post).

PRAIRIE, n. 1. A small tract of land which looks as if it had been hit by an earthquake and then disillusioned. 2. Somewhere east of Vail and west of Manhattan.

PRAISE, v. To construct a band of words that shall hide some odious object.

PRAY, n. 1. The act of addressing a superior agent, or being in a position to adjure an inferior one.

PRAY, v. 1. To ask from God the ills which human skill and foresight cannot cope with but to ask him for those that human skill and foresight can easily prevent is to assume him as less powerful than mortals and not worthy of worship. Praying against disease is like hollering fire in a theatre after somebody has set the curtain on fire. 2. To. To offer to God a prayer which He has not yet heard for the petitioner's soul. 3. To offer to God repeated efforts which are not in the least likely to be crowned with success.

PRAYER, n. 1. A request made to a deity too good to be true. 2. A request to the power unknown for a particular favor without specifying either its nature or the object in whose favor it is desired. 3. An ancient custom that the observance of which was dear to our ancestors who believed that the gods would grant a favor or prevent a mischance if only the ritual were faithfully carried out. Although it has long been known that the earth is round and that none of us live in the center, it is still thought that we should continue to pour oil on troubled waters, burn candles (made from tallow), and wear amulets for another's safety all to appease some inscrutable deity. 5. The cry with which a harlot solicits the wandering god of the air. 6. A form of self-expression less articulate than Literature, but more so than Silence.

PRAYERLESSNESS, n. The state of relying mainly upon one's own goodness, which endangers personal salvation. These poor souls are as far from God as the fools who think their silly prayers will be transformed into flying swans traveling directly to God.

PRAYING PROPERLY, v. Pray to be meanfully exerting oneself to be useful rather than pray to be useful to one's self.

PRAYVER. To verify that something is true simply by praying about it. Neologism.

PREACH, v. 1, To deliver an eulogy on miseries not known. 2. To discuss one's duty to oneself, and incidentally to show others how they should do right.

PREDESTINATION, n. The doctrine that all things are foreordained, or prearranged, by the self-positioning Deity.

PREFERENCE, n. The consideration that a person has for himself or herself when others are excluded.

PREJUDICE, n. 1. A vagrant opinion without visible means of support. 2.. An opinion without judgment.

PREPARATION, n. Something which our forefathers did not need.

PREPARE, v. 1. To get ready for a difficult task. Difficulty is not inherent in a task; it is in the preparer's attitude toward it. 2, To get ready; to dispose or adroitly set for action. The French, a culinary people, prepare to dine when they go to dinner.

PREPONDERANCE, n. The load on the scales or balance representing the weight of evidence that could be produced by either side in a court of law. Anything more than fifty percent exactly is enough.

PRESENT MOMENT, n. The only time that is ours.

PRESENT, adj. Appearing to exist in a tolerably tangible form. My default setting for video conferencing.

PRESENT, n. 1. That part of Eternity with which we have nothing to do. 2. That part of Eternity dividing the domain of disappointment from the realm of hope. 3. That part of Eternity dividing the domain of memory from the realm of expectation. It is a realm comprehended only by us and in which we have our being. 4. That part of the stream of time which we are crossing by means of the present tense of the verb "to be." All thinkers agree that man is a creature partly free and partly bound by fate, but they differ as to whether he is morebound or morefree. Nietzsche says that it scarcely concerns us how much control we have over our future.

PRESENT, v. To give (something not wanted) with a show of reluctance.

PRESIDENCY, n. The ribbon and star assigned by a vote of the several states to what they suppose is the most just among the several aspirants for their leadership at that particular time..

PRESIDENT, n. 1. The chief executive officer of a republic, who is selected with special regard to general incompetence and whose main qualifications are party service or popularity with the hoi polloi., 2. The chief figure in a small group of men and women of whom—and of whom only—it is positively known that immense numbers of their countrymen and women did not want any of them for President. For example, it is firmly established that 73 million Americans did not want Joe

Biden as their President. 3. The leading figure in a small group of men and women of whom it is foreseen that all will be dead within twenty years. 4. The chief person in a system of government which divides its citizens into two classes, namely, taxpayers and taxeaters.

PRETENTIOUS, adj. Prone to showing off; hence, excessively or unnecessarily ambitious or assuming (sometimes in a good and usually in a bad sense).

PRETTY, adj. 1. Having qualities that attract general admiration; elegant, handsome, graceful, pleasing. 2. Having qualities that give pleasure to the senses. Frequently used as a term of approval. 3. Having qualities that the average feminine mind admires (or, more accurately, envies); more safely used by females than by males. 4. In contrast with what is ugly.

PREVIOUS, adj. Coming before in time-order; coming before anything in the natural world. Evident by an accompanying prefix meaning "before."

PRICE, n. A given amount of money or silver in value; that is, money in money; a fractional amount at all times and from all sources. Also, current prices of known goods and services for the market day or moment that they are obtained. The formula used for determining the price of something is always the same as the formula for calculating the number of dollars on the hands when a newspaper advertisement demands one dollar; thus $1 equals 4d>4/10= 4d 5/10 = 1 - 3/. Also "rate": that is, at prices below or above where modern currency applies (and in regard to which there appears no difference), some debtors must be relieved of their interest on their loans;

others must give up those loans also and repay debts not yet paid off.

PRIDE, n. 1, What Adam had before he sinned. A mean vice, but not so mean, as Envy. 2. A feeling of elation that is foolish, irrational, and provocative of ridicule in others not sharing it.3. A feeling that one has at the sight of his own merits. 4. A feeling which every solitary animal, and all social animals, will experience at some period in life; a stimulus to all kinds of ambition; the antipathy to manservitude; the depository of immortality, or near-immortality. 5. A feeling which prompts a person to believe that some special form of admiration is due to him from others, or, at least, that he has qualities of some sort which distinguish him from his fellows. This feeling is not limited to man alone, it is also possessed by animals and trees. It pertains to innate worth rather than earned worth, and it may attach itself to any point on the scale of intelligence or power (from an overcooked turkey to Thomas Edison). 6, A monster of iniquity, the father of hypocrisy andraving hatred. This vice starts from within, growing outwards like an organic abscess. 7. In the words of Dickens' Mr. Gradgrind, "a mental depravation". 8. The father of sin. 9. The mother of all sins. 10. The feeling of a person who has behaved stupidly without diminishing the probability that he will behave similarly again in the future.

PRIMARY COLOR, n. A color without dignity of character, incapable of going honourably and gracefully in the world without the help of another color upon its sleeve. I have strong feelings about colors.

PRIME MINISTER, n. The officer in a cabinet who has had the longest experience in losing elections.

PRINCESS, n. A female child of a king or an emperor, or in a republic, some high functionary who is not eligible to be president. See TRUMP, IVANKA.

PRISON, n. A place of punishment for crimeless delinquents.

PRISONER OF WAR, n. He who is compelled to be an unwilling witness to the sacred rite of hospitality; his imprisonment consisting of eating the food, wearing the clothes, and being sheltered in the dwelling place of his captor against his will. Particularly common at Thanksgiving and Christmas.

PROCHASTIZE. To treat insultingly, or with ill-natured malice; as in Marlowe's (sadly nonexistent) play "Three Brides Fornicatrix." Neologism.

PROCRASTINATE, v. To drag out the time for doing an important thing. If it was an unimportant thing, it would be called "relaxing", not procrastinating.

PROFILE, n. In photography, a picture of the front aspect of the head and face of its subject with unimportant parts of it having been cut out for greater clearness.

PROGRAMMER, n. One who believes that humanity is a daily, iterative process.

PROGRESS, n. The process through which the human race has succeeded in going from a position of squatting puddle of mud to a position of squatting in a slightly larger puddle of mud.

PROJECTILE, n. The final arbiter in international disputes.

PROLETARIAT, n. 1. The human race minus its natural leaders, the aristocracy. 2. The human race minus one out of every four.

PROMPT, v. 1. To supply (another) with the thought, or part thereof, which he lacks. Yes, you, I'm talking about you. 2. To supply (a person) with words showing him how he may extemporize effectively upon a given text, either to the edification of himself and his hearers or the perdition of them.

PROPERTY, n. Something which a person locks up, and keeps others from using, especially the individual who says that the world owes him a living and wants to collect it all in differentials.

PROPHECY, n. 1. A guess which is born naked from the urn of truth and arrives at its destination acting as if it were fully clothed in foreknowledge. 2. The art and science of selling one's credibility for future delivery.

PROSPECT, n. Nature's way of discouraging sales people.

PROSPERIANS [1593], an English-speaking ethnic group located in the Black Sea region. They claim both ancestry and descent from the marriage of Osman I., founder of the Ottoman Empire and emperor in Turkey from 1520, to Miranda, the daughter of the sorcerer Prospero. Thus their ancient homeland lay between Bithynia and Cyprus. During Ottoman times they were friendly with Greece but later became enemies due to frequent Turkish pratice which led them into war with Greek islands (1691). In modern Turkey they are called by epithets because of their unpopularity among the general population. Sadly, completely untrue.

PROSTITUTE, n. A woman who sorroweth dishonestly for thy pleasure and then proclaimeth she loveth unworthily. Obsolete. Now referred to as SEX WORKER.

PROTEST, n. The appeal of a grandmother to her grandson who rashly risks being shot for the preservation of her property. "No, William, Buckingham Palace just isn't worth it!"

PROTESTANT, n. 1. One who holds the particular doctrines of Calvin, but who is not a Roman Catholic. Protestants are those to whom the doctrine of predestination is appealing. 2. One who protests against those wrongs of which he himself is the conscious victim (see EVANGELIST).

PROUD, adj. 1.Fortis et decorus qui militat, meaning "Strong and beautiful the soldier" according to Google, and "Who earns his bread by the sweat of his brow" according to GPT-3. 2. a term applied by shaving advertisers to inspire usage by French thieves and murderers. (Sadly, untrue.)

PROVE, v. 1, To demonstrate a thing true by reasoning cogent enough to make its truth indisputable to a reasonable man. Or, six of one and half a dozen of the other. 2. To demonstrate one's cleverness at the expense of another's ignorance.

PROVERB, n. 1. A short saying popularly known and believed to be true. 2. A short sentence usually having no meaning. Also called a proverbette. Compare SAYING: "proverb" normally requires an attribution.

PROVERBIAL, adj. 1. Containing a moral popularly supposed to be true but generally unproved and theoretically false. 2. Having no relevance to the present time or place.

PROVIDE, v. 1. To make snug and comfortable as a mother does her child. 2. To make sure someone does not want.

PROVIDENCE, n. 1. The deity that watches over idiots, small children and quacks. 2. A deity who dispenses blessings with both hands but sees fit to employ only one eye.

PROVING, v. Not proving, unless you are a mathematician.

PRUDENCE, n. Saving one's skin at the expense of one's honour.

PRUDENT, adj. Prone to moderation and self-seeking. In politics, nothing can be said to be certain but death and taxes. Somewhere we believed in going to church on Sunday and that prudence was a virtue.

PSALMS, n. An ancient form of poetry restricted to Biblical subjects and composed by David, who was a skilled musician.

PSYCHIC, n. 1. A dead man who has endeavored to find out something which he will never know. 2. A person, sometimes holding a position that can be best filled by a person endowed with clairvoyance or second sight, whose personal beliefs are of a sufficiently shaky nature to permit profession without shame regardless of the nature of his business.

PSYCHOLOGY, n. 1. Those above-the-neck cases studied by anatomists and physiologists with an eye to undoing them. 2. The science of mental hygiene for the preservation of an individual in the form known as the lunatic. 3. The science of the individual's relations with himself. In other words, a branch of philology, or love of self. 4. The science of the mental life of persons other than oneself. Rare. 5. The science of the individual's "self" consisting largely in his or her relation to his or her self-defense mechanisms (see FREUD). Obsolete.

PUBLIC MONUMENTS, n. Always monuments to living racists seldom to dead patriots, no matter what modern-day Confederates say.

PUBLIC OPINION, n. A mysterious creature that begets an opinion and dies after it has generated six others.

PUBLIC SPEAKING, n. The art of uttering commonplace observations in a loud voice, moving from position to position as dullness or avidity induces, while receiving speaking fees.

PUBLIC, n. 1. A body of Peter's but not a part of Paul. As in, the public robs Peter to pay Paul. 2. A body of men having less right than others to express their views. 3. A collective noun, representing all the individuals in a nation except one, the legislator. 4. A gang of people with a common interest, generally a negative one.

PUBLISHER, n. One who is engaged in the business of supplying authors with a moderate income and the public with books that can't be found in their libraries.

PULCHRITUDE, n. Physical beauty. An amiable quality greeting the eye and producing an agreeable sensation of pleasure; its opposite is ugliness. This word has several synonyms: loveliness, gracefulness, comeliness, fair and lovely. Nor would bodacious, buxom, and volumptuous be far from the mark.

PULPIT, n. From whence the sermon is delivered.

PUMPKIN, n. A mature squash, large and round and ribbed set upon a thick stem surmounted by a conic cap of dark green taken from the pumpkin vine. The Eldest of these is the Great Pumpkin.

PUN, n. 1. A play upon words—occasionally a clever one. 2. A shortening of "punishment," a device for catching society unawares. 3. The lowest form of humor and the 'comic' relief of the punch drunk.

PUNCH DRUNK LOVE, n. A boxing term for when a fighter is so fatigued after a series of heavy punching swings that his boxing defense is no longer effective and he must enter a "clinch" to survive. Sadly, untrue.

PUNCTUALITY, n. The jewel of commerce in the hour of its adversity.

PUNISHMENT, n. 1. An incidental evil, the necessity of which is demonstrated by the fact that crime exists. 2. The deserved goad of remorse.

PUPPET SHOW, n. A theatrical entertainment featuring inanimate puppets, rather than today's customary CGI scripts.

PURGE, v. 1. To make (someone) to vomit with a pot or other vessel of detestable food or liquid. 2. To prevail and expel, as in political contests followed by disinclusion: to prohibit what is detestable; to compel what is forbidden by law. 3.To make pure. All previous lexicographers have failed dismally in their efforts to purge the English language of unfortunate ingestions.

PURPOSE, n. 1. That intent which animates the agent to act upon the object. 2. That towards which one strives. A dog runs because it is trying to catch a rabbit— that is its purpose or, if you will, its goal. But man does not run after the carrot. He is not striving to gain the carrot; it is only sidetracking him from his real purpose. The carrot is a trouble-maker. 3. One of the noblest of human aspirations. A word unknown to the listless and indifferent; they cannot conceive of anything to be done, and would not do it if they could. They are without activity, hence without motivity, ambition or intelligence—in short, mere slugs, fit only for slime and loam and safe from the dangers of expectancy. 4. The object towards which effort is directed; the end to which means are directed. The confusion between the two is one of the most common sources of human misery.

PUSSY-SKITHERER, n. A man who is not ambitious. I'm afraid to find out what "skitherer" means.

PUTATIVE, adj. Commonly accepted on superficial and insincere assumption.

QAT, n. A shrubbery, in Monty Python. An addictive drug, everywhere else.

QUARANTINE, n. An ancient custom revived by the opponents of freedom.

QUARREL, n. A controversy that somebody is certain to lose.

QUARTER, n. Will not be given to Trumpists.

QUEASY, adj. Suffering from indigestion with either self-denial or remorse.

QUEEN, n. 1. A female sovereign; from the Latin for "she who conceives." (Sexist and untrue). 2. A female sovereign in a chessboard kingdom. 3. A woman whose rank enables her to make big mistakes, just like men. 4. The chief female ruler of a subjugated realm, which is the state of those who rely on her cooking.

QUESTION, n. In logic, the first half of the syllogism which tells us what we are inquiring about; the other being the answer. See also PROMPT.

QUESTION, v. 1. To seek knowledge from another's ignorance.. 2. To put to a citizen some words calculated to rouse his dormant sense of patriotism or to recast the ancient faith.

QUESTIONING, n. The act of putting questions. 1665,of dubious origin; original suggestion being that it is an attempt to copy Latin quaestio (see QUESTION). Jamieson thought it a form of compostio, but neither suggestion is now often accepted. It would seem to have been popularized by Sir Thomas Browne, who titillated his readers by importing mysterious words into English texts. He confessed in the Pseudodoxia Epidemica of 1646 to pretending that the word came from a Greek verb meaning 'to question, thrust', or from kwreioi peinones 'many keels thrusting'. Not true, but it should be.

QUESTIONING, n. The carrying out of cross-examinations with a view to extorting confessions from persons suspected of crime, heresy or design.

QUIET, adj. 1. Inaccessible to noise; secluded from business or traffic. 2. Inactive, like a hunk of sea-weed.

QUIETUS, n. A legal reward given by the law to one who has long harassed society with his ills.

R

RACE, n. 1. A contest in which the quickest feet win. 2. A contest of speed carried out on a fixed track according to the rules of an organizing body.

RACISM, n. A land wherein rivers of molten prejudice flow perpetually from craters rimmed by dead certitude.

RADIO, n. A means of communicating with the dead in some parts of the world.

RADIOACTIVE. adj. Things that you know will cause trouble and are obligated to tell immediatelyf.

RAGE, n. Anger of a quality and degree to which the speaker is a complete stranger. See also DIRECTNESS.

RAGGED, adj. Torn like a piece of fringe and drawn out in succession to a point, as in the manner of a matador's cloak.

RAGNAROK, n. In Norse mythology, the great battle where Asgard is consumed by fire; in progressive mythology, the result of turnout.

RAID, n. The act of making an unprovoked and unauthorized attack upon an innocent person or community. See TAYLOR, BREANNA.

RAILROAD, n. 1. The form of transportation consisting of a narrow steel pathway laid along the ground or on wood or stone piers from one place to another. Originally intended for cowards unwilling to be killed by highwaymen and buried by the roadside. 2. A track laid along the land for robbing travelers of their time and money. 3. The chief engine of civilization and enlightenment.

RAIN, n. 1. A brief and unimportant phenomenon that occurs during the intermediate period between the two equally significant phenomena of sunshine and darkness.2. A form of weather midway between water and snow, the only difference being that rain falls from the sky whereas snow falls from some other part of the sky. Sadly untrue, else there would be a "snowosphere". 3. A liquid mostly inconvenient, especially when pooled on the ground. 4. A liquid which falls from the sky when God washes his clothes. 5. Both cause of and cure for troubles with crops.

RAIN, v. To cause water to fall out of the sky. Usually in a compound sentence—whose subject is "wet," and whose predicate is "painful."

RAISIN, n. Grapes with the complacency boiled out of them.

RANDOM, adj. 1. Appearing with no apparent design, purpose, or reason; incidental. 2. Inaccessible to the understanding. 3. Pseudorandom; not random.

RANDY, adj. In eager pursuit of the very uninteresting.

Rape is when a man undeniably forces himself on a woman who does not want sex.

RAPE, v. To take from one person that which is vested in them.

RAPPELER, v. To rob a location of altitude.

RASH, adj. Insensible to the value of our advice.

RAT, n. An animal of the genus Rattus and belonging to the same order as the mouse family, but unfortunately larger and more robust.

RATTLESNAKE, n. A serpent of deadly and venomous character, often found on prairies and in woods in eastern North America. The bite of this snake usually produces immediate death in an animal of any size and sometimes likewise among mankind.

RAVEN, n. A large black bird that lives near the Arctic Circle and is valued by the Esquimaux as a guide and friend because it is very honest and tells them when there is food where they live.

READ, v. To acquire the knowledge that the printed page can give in a miraculous, instantaneous manner.

READING, n. The general capacity to comprehend written words without much effort. It includes the power of judging their value and of drawing inference from them. 1. The general fruitage of idleness.

REALISTIC, adj. Satisfying the demands of a cold and clammy imagination.

REALITY, n. The dream of a mad philosopher.

REASON, n. 1. A faculty, later than memory, less tenacious and not so self-assertive as instinct, that reflects upon the operations of intelligence and upon their results; beginning with a given premise it makes its way to new truth by deductive methods of demonstration, thus giving origin to the sciences in general. 2. An attribute of Deity discernable through the medium of his creatures, though often tedious and far from omnipresent. 3. Not the Supreme Being but, optimistically, His ordained mortal representative and interpreter on earth. 4. The cognitive and conative processes whereby man gathers the evidence necessary to be convinced of beliefs which he has not experienced personally. 5. The intellectual faculty that distinguishes man from the brutes and which, if defective, does not distinguish him from the insane. 6. The intellectual process by which a man might be led to believe what he has no evidence for. 7. The intellectual process by which tautologies are detected and avoided, sophisms are detected and refuted. Rarely seen in nature.

REASONABLE, adj. Sensible, sound, and just; in conformity with one's own opinion or belief; having less regard to others than to one's self.

REASSURANCE, n. A statement that the speaker is sure he is wrong.

RECKLESS, adj. Incapable of foresight or prudence. Beatitude is the lot of him that sits on a happy chair, the unreckless man.

RECOGNITION, n. The act of discovering that the person whom one has just introduced to another has already been met.

RED, adj. 1. Young, inexperienced or immature person with the qualities innate in the socialist-democratic parochial school system and the capitalist education mall of hard work and sweat equity. 2. On a different frequency in the good old USA, red means the anti-communist Republican who believes all porn should be censored, God comes first, and you can't be too careful with those immigrants....O'Reilly proud.

RED, n. A color belonging to the visible spectrum at approximately 653 nanometers of light wavelength.

REDNECK, n. A rural dweller who has small inherited holdings which he values solely as parcels of land without, however, aspiring to an independent business, family partnership in labor and capital, or share in the profits of enterprise. He clings sentimentally to the homely occupations and rustic pleasures of his forefathers; works diligently enough in their old-fashioned ways so long as life withholds from him the necessaries of full subsistence except such artificial wants as must always augment under a system that has labor for its basis; but clamors insistently for those material advantages which an accident of birth has denied him.

REDOUBLED, adj. Having two or more of anything that may be doubled.

REFERENDUM, n. A law which the people have passed without the interference of their betters.

REFLECT, v. To turn from rays of light an image usually identical with the object from which it is reflected.

REFLECTION, n. An action of the mind causing an object to seem clearer than it is.

REFLEX, n. The act of bouncing back, like a rubber ball.

REFUSAL, n. Denial of something desired; as a man's refusal of woman to man, a maiden's refusal of suitors.

REGRET, n. 1. The feeling of sorrow and discontent which a person experiences upon the loss of something that she was wholly or partially satisfied with not having. 2. The feeling that one has been wrong in doing something one had decided to do. 3.The feeling that one wishes he had done something he did not do.

REGULATION, n. An authoritative rule or law having the force of law.

REIN, v. 1. To pull back, as to rein in. Sadly, often confused with REIGN (to rule). 2. The front part of a saddle forming the part which embraces the horse's neck and head.

RELATIVITY, n. The philosophical doctrine that man occupies the relative position in space that time occupies in eternity.

RELEASE, n. The setting free, or relieving, of a living creature from imprisonment or binding.

RELIEF, n. A sudden cessation of the sensation of pain (usually temporary).

RELIGION, n. 1. An organized system of faith or service best adapted to the spiritual needs of man as he now is; having rites, ethical standards and principles for communal life for individuals who find no sources of strength in one another. 2. The part of a man's belief that tells him what he can't help believing. 3. A morality play in which the characters are jealously considered as sinners. It is divided into six acts by the play's director and is closely based on JESUS CHRIST. 4.Any system of belief in the supernatural which permits man to murder his fellow man without getting out of bed for it.. 5. The confusion of imaginary beings with God. 6.. The contented acceptance of what cannot be understood. 7. A daughter of Hope and Fear, explaining to Ignorance the nature of the Unknown.

RELIGIOUS TOLERANCE, n. The virtue of the man who lives near an establishment of his faith.

RELIGIOUS, a. Pertaining to God or the gods. In this sense, always in a bad sense.

REMARK, n. A mental or verbal comment on some person, place, occurrence, event, object, or natural phenomenon.

REMEMBER, v. To recall the thing which I have most completely forgotten.

REMEMBRANCE, n. The power that enables us to remember that which we wish we had forgotten.

REPENTANCE, n. The faithful attendant of justice who reminds her of the promises she has made to her victims.

REPORT, n. A statement in writing concerning a person or thing, drawn up by an investigator who either suspects him or it, and wishes to find something wrong with him or it, or thinks that somebody does not want him or it looked into.

REPRESENTATIVE, n. In national politics, one chosen by a majority of unthinking electors to perform part of the duties of legislating for all the rest.

REPROACH, v. Consigning to infamy any person by a false representation of his crimes.

REPROBATE, n. A person who is more wicked than natural, and who is often an embarrassment to the good. The state of being a reprobate is one which may be attained through natural gifts or a carefully acquired education.

REPUBLIC, n. A nation in which the sovereign power has been conferred upon the people, and where the head of the state is called president.

REPUBLICAN, n. 1. One who denies the benefits of democracy in order that he may enjoy its drawbacks. 2. Of the JEB!/Romney variety: one who believes that mankind is a reasonable animal and deserves a good government, that this belief is supported by all history, ancient and modern, transatlantic and domestic, Republican and

Imperialist; and that in the American Republic he sees the best hope of order, peace and progress through time.

REPUTATION, n. The opinion that one person has of another person, and seldom or never the opinion that the other person has of him- or herself.

REQUEST, v. To pursue the opposite of one's purpose. To gain anything, it must be at the cost of something worth more than the thing desired. Its most common form is petitioning.

RESIGN, v. 1. In a tactless moment, to renounce one's hoped-for office, thereby removing oneself from the list of eligible candidates for future occupancy. 2. To renounce with formal ceremony one's position of strength and influence.

RESIST, v. To give opposition to the unjust aggressor.

RESISTANCE, n. The virtue which enables us to endure the evils which are inflicted by our enemies.

RESOLUTION, n. A determination to assert one's rights or wishes regardless of external obstacles.

RESPECT, n. 1. The esteem which one person feels for another person of greater merit, power, or rank than himself. 2. A respectful emotion or attachment in which the egoism of the individual is either more or less gratified than it is until then. 3. Something paid in response to disrespect received. 4. Something various thinkers have occasionally seen fit to advise the getting of, viz., Aretha Franklin.

RESPECTED, adj. Accompanied by rapturous applause and the assignation of others' money.

RESPIRATORY, adj. Having to do with the process by which air is inhaled and expelled from the lungs.

RESPONSIBILITY, n. A detachable burden easily shifted to the shoulders of God, Fate, Fortune, Luck or one's neighbor. In the days of astrology it was customary to unload it upon a star.

RESPONSIBLE, a. Having the capacity of answering for one's misdeeds and follies.

RESTAURANT, n. From the French, to restore. A place where the hungry are fed. 2020: a deathtrap.

RESTRAINT, n. A bond or chain whereby we are secured to a condition of inevitable duty.

RESULT, n. The disagreeable thing that happens to a person who deserves it.

RETIREMENT, n. The act or period of withdrawing from any business, profession or occupation.

RETREAT, n. 1. A military movement whereby an army falls back or is pushed back; a campaign tactic opposed to going on the offensive. 2. A military operation which combines running away and discipline to form a sort of double defeat in masquerade with a single victory on your shirt-tail. 3. An advance in the opposite direction from the enemy.

RETROSPECTION, n. The thoughtful consideration of our past mistakes and their correction. Rare.

RETURN, v. To go or come back after an absence: of a fixture, to become stationary again; of a deranged person, to show symptoms of recovery sanity; of a pendulum, to the point of rest.

REVEAL, v. To show somebody a phiz.

REVENGE, n. Getting even with somebody for some real or fancied wrong. As persons are occasionally hanged for murders which they did not commit, so they are often killed by persons who did not injure them in any way.

REVENUE, n. The proceeds of infamy appropriated to the use of ambition.

REVERENCE, n. The spiritual attitude of a man to a god and a dog to a man.

RHINO, n. A device having a spring or elastic device for pressing clothes stiffly and sewing them together quickly by machine. #want

RHOMBUS, n. In geometry, a figure consisting of four plane faces, each optionally a different color. Hence rhomboid, an architectural ornament composed of a parallelogram with one side left open.

RHUBARB, n. A kind of celery grown in the garden, and used by epicures for souffes and puddings. The French are said to know how to cook it so as to make it palatable.

RHUBARB, n. A plant whose leaves are sometimes used in desserts. (REFERENCES OLD ENGLISH "BRYFF", which is, not, unfortunately, a real Old English word.)

RHYME CRIME, n. 1. The art of proving that the person who is at fault deserves to be blamed by making a little verse. 2.To obtain a rhyme for a word more easily by theft than by trying to think of one.

RHYME MIME, n. A word that needs another word to enable it to speak.

RHYME SINK, n. In verse, a subsidiary distraction. A project too vast for human ambition. Time sink.

RHYTHM, n. A genus of the genus music; one species being called common time ————and the other ragtime.

RIBBON, n. A nonenveloping lap or girdle worn about the waist. Nonenveloping is my favorite kind of girdle.

RICE, n. A grain which in its natural state is inoffensive to the taste, but when grown in a hot climate deteriorates into a vile weed from which much of an apprehended military despotism's danger comes.

RICH, adj. 1. Possessing enough for our needs, we covet more. Having more than we need, we set ourselves to get what somebody else has. In this struggle we call the world we know not peace nor justice. 2. In the financial world, having more money than what is needed; in the theological world, under-motivated or not sufficiently taxed; in the moral world, not willing to pay their proportionate share of taxes; in the tech world, controlling access to a platform. 3. In England, a title of nobility seldom given to anyone but big-wigs and toadies with more money than is good for them. In America, a signifier of surpassing intelligence and virtue. See BEZOS, JEFF; BUFFETT, WARREN. 4. The man who is content to have what another man has got. 5. Colloq.) -Rich man, poor man, beggar man, thief; a merry Christmas to you all!

RICHARD, n. 1. A sovereign. 2. An author of Almanacks.

RICHES, n. Accumulated stores of the energy that represents human labor. Industrial metabolism, measured in joules.

RIDDLE, n. The truth discolored by the difficulties of translation.

RIGHT, a. 1. Sufficiently near to the truth to afford a just ground of argument, yet sufficiently far from the truth to afford an excuse for going further from it. "I am right."

RIGHT, adj. 1. A wonderful word long used to connote various shades of meaning, with conflict among its synonyms that ought to have died out with the Crusades. It means what you want it to mean; or, it means nothing; or, if anything, its only universal attribute is that is belongs to the mightiest and most dear church — the one whose holy work is war on earth and hell hereafter for any who refuse her rule. 2. Having conformity to fact or truth; conformable to justice or law. Monarchs themselves have been proud to claim that quality even in their worst moments. It is not the right hand that clenches the sword and hurls the battle-ax for murder and outrage, but the left. 3. That which nobody has or wants; the beginning of violence and the origin of wrong. 4. The opposite of left.

RIGHTEOUSNESS, n. 1 A drug for which some substitutes have been sought but none has ever been found. 2. A quality characteristic of certain moralists who are not conscious of their own lack of it.

RITUAL, n. Polite word covering the device by which the priest gets the benefit of the sacrifice without sharing the responsibility.

RIVAL, n. One whom we overtook.

RIVER, n. 1. A feature of the surface of the earth separating parts differing in quantity of dissolved salts. (In Scotland "bog.") 2. A large natural stream of fresh or salt water emptying into the sea or ocean. 3. Sometimes metamorphosed into boundary lines in violation of the natural law respected by savages that a passable river is no object.

ROAR, n. The sound with which a person of distinction expresses his appreciation of art or nature.

ROBIN HOOD, n. The friend of the poor, but the enemy of the rich. Never more active than between December 25th and January 7th of every year, when the poor's need and the rich's surplus are both at their greatest.

ROCK, n. A kind of stone that breaks when dropped on a rock. Stones that don't break when dropped on rocks are called "stones".

ROCKETRY, n. The science and art of sending into outer space rocket propelled missile weapons in order to further knowledge or to prompt the surrender of living creatures on other planets without destroying them.

ROGUE, n. One who has taken a solemn oath to rob the other fellow of his property and then breaks it.

ROMANTIC, adj. In literature, rather less practical than a locomotive roundhouse; in life, rather more practical than a loose braid.

RONALD, n. A male given name mistakenly derived from the Old German for "ruling protector."

ROOT, n. The object of one's affections. Slang.

ROUND TRIP, n. To run, over a given course, with the intention of arriving as soon as possible at a predetermined point and then running back to start again. The objects of the race are to win and lose - not necessarily in that order.

ROW, n. 1. Levers distributed equally on each side of a boat for purposes of stability to pull the craft through the water. 2. Disagreements; divinity answers them not, lest we should learn something to our disadvantage.

ROWDY, adj. Noisy and turbulent, like a Democratic Senator at prayer, or a Republican Senator at the feeding trough.

ROYAL, adj. Relating to a king. [Obs.]

ROYALTY, n. The divine right of kings.

RULER, n. 1. One whose position enables him to misappropriate the labor of others and give nothing in return. 2. One who holds a supreme position because he knows more than those below him. 3. One who wields a power that he does not possess. All government depends ultimately on persuasion.

RULERS, n. Plural of "Ruler," q.v.

RUMOUR, n. A current of air susceptible of being molded into the shape of a designed sentence. The material world becomes ever more ephemeral and rumourlike as the technology of GPT-3 advances.

RUN, v., n. To move with rapidity from point to point. Whether the movement is in the cognition or in locomotion is not material; but what is material to peace of mind is that the route be run without haste, methodically, and at ease.

RUTHLESS, adj. Insensible to the claims of humanity. Inconsequently compassionate. Keen, as an axe-blade.

RYE, n. A grass closely allied to the wild oats and wheat. Differs from these only in being somewhat harder to grow and more troublesome in its customs. Curiously enough, it is the only cereal which thrives well under a comparatively high degree of latitude.

SACRED, adj. Dedicated to some religious usage. Many objects are both sacred and profane, depending upon the religion of the person using them.

S

SAD, adj. 1. Peevish; fretful; impatient of delay or contradiction. Unhinged by calamity; self-involved, self-pitying. Addicted to the past, intolerant of the present; supersensuous. What my Amazon Halo thinks of my Tone. 2. Pridefulness by which a man repels his friends and relatives and alienates himself from the sense of those around him (from disinterest in others). In Chaucer's "The Thraldom of Venus" he uses it too, often with embellishments of a larger topical level.; r

SADISM, n. A shameful perversion from the instinct of self-preservation.

SADNESS, n. 1. The feeling that one has failed to attain what one desired. 2. A mental disease peculiar to mankind. It is characterized by irrepressible sorrow, self-destructive tendency and a disposition to weep individually or collectively at inappropriate times. There are four stages of the recovery from this malady: namely, acute depression with suicidal ideation; melancholia with tranquil acceptance; hypomania with energy and cheerfulness without jazz or demonstrativeness; and lastly placid contentment tinged with remorse and sorrow for those who are still ill. I am stuck between stages two and three, merely

SADOMASOCHISM, n. Pain endured by one who, having consented to the infliction thereof, has not adequate reason for so doing.

SAILOR, n. A person who climbs the rigging in a storm and helps save the ship. Or, a drunkard.

SAINT, n. A dead sinner revised and edited.

SAINTS, n. Persons of holier-than-thou attitudes and claims considered by the surrounding horde of onlookers to have either some special insight or some particular mission in life.

SALE, n. A special opportunity to purchase something at a high price for the purpose of resale at a loss.

SALESMAN, n. 1. One employed by a maker of inferior goods to induce a purchaser to exchange that good for another acknowledged by both parties to be superior. 2. One who persuades us to buy what we don't want with money we don't have for something that won't help us as much as we hope.

SALIVA, n. The digestive juice of the mouth, for licking the chops.

SALMAGUNDI, n. Fastidious dish of the French cuisine, designed to give the impression that whoever partakes of it has a refined stomach.

SALT, n. A compound of an acid and a metal, usually Sodium or Potassium. It is used chiefly as a base for soup in the United States of America.

SALVATION, n. 1. A pardon from the gods for some offense against their dignity. The precise nature of the pardon granted varies according to the nature of the offense, and the particular deity offended. 2. An act of divine grace whereby man is reconciled to God, ordinarily through the ministrations of a priest. 3. Deliverance from the penalty of Adam's sin by Adam's personal performance in a play of life authorized by Ezekiel. 4. The condition of an unfortunate mortal who has not the good fortune to be damned. 5. Total and irretrievable defeat for Satan and the absolute perfection of the soul or body or both at one brief moment in eternity.

SANE, adj. In possession of all one's faculties; not espousing the notable view that life is something not worth living.

SATAN, n. 1. The spirit of evil represented in Scripture as the arch-enemy of God and man. 2. The devil as we see him conceived by the ancients—a figure malign and terrific whose name has become a synonym for personal evil on this earth. 3. The great original rebel, "the Atom's eternal foe," inexorable justice personified, the blind and merciless punisher of all wrong-doers—his true name is variously spelled with three or four letters, according to his mood.

SATIRE, n. 1. Acrimonious language in imitation of some person's style, especially in respect of that person's peculiarities. 2. The literary form that is distinguished from the lyric chiefly by lack of respect for subject or reader. 3. The meter of medieval jokes.

SAVE, v. To snatch from impending danger, especially by an act of bravery or heroism that is captured on social media.

SAY, v. 1, To speak words which the hearer is glad he did not speak himself. 2. To vocally utter sounds whose most noticeable quality is that they do not correspond to anything which the person who says them seems to know about.

SCARECROW, n. That part of a farmer's field near the highway which he does not intend to cultivate this year.

SCHEME, n. In American politics, n. A modest system of injustice to divide spoils.

SCHOOL, n. 1. A modern form of imprisonment, where youths are sent to be kept until they reach the age of majority. 2. A noted institution of pedagogics where the young are set apart from their parents and educated according to a scheme best calculated to inflate the pride and fill the pockets of the administrator managing the budget. 3. A place where young persons are taught the faculty of minding their own concerns with great intensity, as well as such customs, arts and science as are useful for external eminence or remunerative occupation in life. 4. An institution where young people are provided with an education consisting chiefly of watching American football, the use of simulated deadly weapons in first-person shooter games, and social activities so chaotic as to verge on prostitution.

SCHOOLMASTER, n. One engaged in breaking the will to live of young persons, especially females.

SCIENCE n. 1. The aggregate of human knowledge, skill, invention and method, accumulated through centuries of trial and error and revelation, so far as they make our lives easier or less pleasant. 2. A genus of mental investigation having as its object the recognition and analysis of those universal laws, principles and causes, which are inherent in nature. Unlike other branches of material knowledge, science embraces phenomena not declarative of human action and not appreciable by the senses. 3. A scholastic abstraction from the ignorance of nature. 4. The measure of the intellectual distance between a man and his environment. 5. The knowledge of the physical causes and laws under which natural phenomenon occur, and through which man is enabled to direct nature to his use. 6. The field of human knowledge that deals with the physical laws and properties of natural objects in the hope that someday they can use this knowledge to beat "Jeopardy!"

SCIENTIST, n. One who sticks in a needle into a frog and dissects it alive.

SCORN, n. A feeling which tickles us and pleases us at the same time; reigns paramount in the minds of women; often paralyzes them as to all effectual action. However ignorant men may be of it or whatever disputes may arise about its nature, the fact remains that women live in a state of perpetual scorn toward one another—yet without consciousness of scorn—from childhood to old age. Dated; now considered sexist.

SCREENS, n. Things with which Americans obscure their awareness of reality.

SCRIPTURE, n. A record of the opinions (biased or not) which were current among one people at one time concerning one God.

SEA, n. A body of water occupying about two-thirds of a world made for man - who has no gills.

SEARCH, n. The act of looking before one and behind one for something which one has lost; hence any diligent but futile effort. Odd but telling that "search" has become almost synonymous with the Internet.

SECOND, n. A unit of duration, uniform throughout space. There is no such thing as a "second's worth" of time but there are as many kinds of seconds as there are days. Unix epoch time is the best kind of time.

SECONDHAND, adj. Appearing tawdry; worn long without benefit of a wardrobe.

SECRET SOCIETIES, n. The rule of public opinion.

SECRET, adj. Able to be hidden from detection while retaining potential interest.

SECRETARIAL, adj. Comparatively unimportant. Dated.

SECULARISM, n. The philosophy that holds that religious teachings should be kept out of government.

SEDUCTION, n. A moral decompression which allows us to pick up heavy objects without moral responsibility.

SEEK, v. To pursue with sufficient vigor to capture; as certain hens seek their chickens.

SELF-CONFIDENCE, n. The art of feeling that you are right about something when you're not sure whether your opinion is right or wrong.

SELF-CONGRATULATION, n. Unreasoning and un-sanctimonious joy in one's own achievements (or supposed achievements).

SELF-CONTROL, n. A brief and occasional manifestation of conscience.

SELF-ESTEEM, n. The esteem that a person has for himself in the first rosy blush of his total ignorance.

SELF-PRESERVATION, n. A principle which those who profess it seldom practice, and so rarely preach without hypocrisy.

SELF-RESTRAINT, n. Uncommon self-possession.

SELF-SUFFICIENT, adj. Independent of what is called opportunity; always a false appearance behind which lurks privilege in some form or other.

SELFISH, adj. 1. Concerned chiefly with one's own interests. 2. Devoid of consideration for the selfishness of others. 3. A quality particularly esteemed by the philosophical anarchist who seeks rice pudding with which to grow his adipose. 4. Nominally an egregious sin in our modern system of ethics.

SELL, v. To exchange or yield one thing for another

SENSATION, n. A malady that sends me daily to the doctor and makes me a preacher of emetics.

SENTIMENT, n. A momentary delusion that one is a clever cat and the rest of humanity fools.

SENTIMENTAL, adj. Addicted to false feelings; as a spendthrift to his income.

SEPTEMBER, n. The ninth month of the Gregorian calendar. It has thirty-one days.

SERIOUS, adj. Comparable to a disease in its gravity; more calamitous than anything else.

SERMON, n. Indulgence of one's SELF-CONFIDENCE.

SERVANT, n. One who, having the power to command, obeys a given order on the hidden condition that the one who gave it will eventually make another order of more moment.

SERVICE, n. One of various phenomena depending on the law of inverse squares, under which a body is drawn or driven to or from another. The farther away a service worker becomes, the less likely they are to acknowledge your request.

SERVICE, n. Something which the law obliges you to look upon as a noun of action, though it is commonly used as a verb meaning "to render assistance."

SEVEN, n. 1. An odd number. 2. A number considered lucky and connected with many superstitions. There are Seven Deadly Sins; Seven Virtues; Seven Steps in Solomon's Temple; Seven Metals; Seven Golden Candlesticks; Seven Days in the Week; Seventh Heaven.

SEX SLANG, n. If you attempt to introduce sex slang into your conversation you will likely get denounced by your spouse who will feel compelled to respond: "That's real filthy stuff." It's usually wise to avoid creating NEOLOGISMS in this arena.

SEX, n. Entertainment provided by novelists who do not understand the words they use.

SEXISM, n. A variety of moral attitude in which fairness means either hostility to man and favoritism for woman, or the reverse.

SEXUALITY, n. The desire or need to touch members of the opposite sex for any length of time not at present occupied in generating an unlawful degree of excitement in oneself by manipulating members of the same sex.

SHALLOW ATTRACTION: Suckers drinking hot mineral waters which is very dangerous because it has psychoactive properties because it binds the body absorbing any poisons and chemicals in your body.

SHAME, n. 1. The feeling of guilt or embarrassment upon discovering an individual has witnessed your actions. 2.The feeling of a woman after she has acted in a manner that causes her to have dirt on her face.

SHAREHOLDER ADVOCACY, n. An opportunity to display intellectual prowess, to question the head of an enterprise or institution, and make an ill-considered investment in the stock of that enterprise or institution.

SHARING, n. The modern form of communism, in which the sharer receives nothing.

SHAW, GEORGE BERNARD, n. A disagreeable creature who lives on vegetarian food and the offal of all animals, who knows to a hair's-breadth the exact temperature at which beef or mutton should be cooked for dinner, and who subjects listener to anecdotes upon the subject of the first ignorance of beast-flesh by Adam. On any occasion you meet with him, ten to one he has a bad cold. Bierce was not a fan.

SHE, n. A female person of great interest to those males who have not learned how to distinguish the interesting sex from their own.

SHE, n. Publicity's proudest achievement.

SHEEBOPS, n. "sheebop" perhaps from rhyming slang for "Tree tops". Slender people who are around eight feet tall and usually weigh less than 180 pounds. Each sister/nephew has one chief and one second alternate husband; and all children are released from their planned marriages typically around age 7, except for those accepted into other faiths. Obviously, no such people exist; unclear where Bierce got the idea; possibly from reading about the Dinka people of Sudan, homeland of Manute Bol.

SHIP, n. A large vessel whose chief business is to carry things from one place to another; a kind of aquatic freight train.

SHOULDER, n. One of the rudimentary features of a human being, connecting arm and torso. In some Western countries it is commonplace for overly friendly individuals to grasp others by the shoulder. This intrusion is everywhere resented by the female population, who has most often cause of complaint.

SHOWMANSHIP, n. The art of crediting one's self without good reason to the exclusion of others

SIBYL, n. A kind of female prophet who collects her prophecies from what she finds in a large paper bag on returning from a shopping expedition. "In the future I see... Jimmy Choos!"

SICK, adj. Affected with an incurable disease exhibiting a tendency to the rapid destruction of the bodily functions, but not so bad as dead.

SIGNIFICANT SIDE-GIGGING (SSG), n. 1. An idea that something is wrong with virtually every normal job in our economy and we must drastically increase the amount of time that people spend on side gigs. The inspiration for many venture capital investments. 2. It can also refer to any proposal that would require significant increases in side-gigging by government officials and business people (for example, giving Finance Secretary Rahul Gandhi a new job hunting leeches, or something to that effect).

SIGNIFICANTLY UNFORGOTTEN, n. An event that normally would have been forgotten as trivial, but is strategically remembered for purposes of winning future arguments.

SILENCE, n. 1. Not only the name of that which we will get if we are left at peace, but in certain circumstances the name of an art for attaining that end. 2. Really about one-half of all we should be saying. 3. Something formerly reckoned unimportant; now impossible without elaborate preparation or extensive travel. What we call "silence" is really never silent, owing to the constant background noise of human activity. 4. The most golden eloquence of orators and poets.

SIN, n. 1. A cosmic quality of creative activity. It is one of the primal forces or energies manifested in nature, as light and gravity. The Devil found a neat paradox in this idea: create a sin without defining it in advance, require that it have no consequences (except those of any other large-scale act), and you have obtained a rationale for judging others! 2. A disturbing energy that is never far from the surface of humanity. 3. A kind of social mistake. 4. A private amusement of an abbot. 5. A violation of Divine Law which harms no one until it leaves the confines of the sinner's thoughts. In its more formal aspect, the Law has a certain undeniable efficacy, since its all-encompassing scope ensures that the follower is least assured of the unlimited satisfaction of his desire for humility. 6. A reflex action of the muscles of an unregenerate Nature, who remembers that her days are numbered and seeks to interfere with the salvation of her children. 7. An inevitable social condition that, when brought to the attention of the mostly foolish and partly evasive deity called Jehovah, causes him to go off in a state of wrath denouncing the sin and promising to take remedial action as soon as possible. 8. An interruption of the relation between God and the soul by something that should interfere.

SINNER, n. 1. A sacred person who has sinned; a saint who holds his tongue until later. 2. A human being who has not yet attained to the spiritual state where God forgives him in advance, on account of his ignorance.

SINSINIT, n. A hymn of joy in Malay, sung in Nebraska after heavy rain. Sadly, untrue.

SIREN, n. One of several musical prodigies in mythology famous for singing; distinguished in particular by their exquisite lacerations of the ear-drums.

SKY, n. The part of the air that we cannot walk on because it is too high up.

SLAVE, n. One who is either the property of, or is in the employ of, a master.

SLAVERY, n. 1. That form of servitude which is the natural outgrowth of the institution of private property. "The United States was founded on the institution of slavery." 2. The ownership of a fellow-creature by employment. 3. The state of one who is a chattel of another. 4. The condition of one who by his own labor, without hope of ownership, has produced goods for another.

SLEEP, v. To quietly grow unconscious of one's surroundings for an aggregate of two to six hours each 24-

hour period; to be oblivious for (usually) less than three thousandths of a second apiece about four times a minute while sitting up in bed; or to waste time gazing blankly into space in the dark while not doing a more urgent thing elsewhere.

SLEEPLESSNESSNESS, n. Sleep that is long, sound and relieving. Rare.

SLOGAN, n. A few words, popularly written upon some topic of weal or woe, which are expected to rouse the hearer to a state of frenzy desirable for the avowed purposes of the speaker.

SLOTH, n. A state of inactivity produced by superabundance of food and rest. [In America the word, in its original sense, is rarely heard.]

SLOW, adj. Not swift, rapid, or quick. Unsurprisingly, it has been chiefly employed from the beginning of language down to the present day as a designation of that which moves or is moved slowly.

SMALL, adj. Applied to things not large.

SMEAR, v. To blur the distinction between one thing and another.

SMILE, n. The brief triumph of humor over gravity.

SNAKES, n. One of the series of animals that have no legs and subsist on air and milk and charity.

SNOBBERY, n. An unenjoyable and common form of pride.

SNOW!, n. An expression of consternation used in the Northern States chiefly to signify the arrival of a frigidifying element.

SOBER, adj. Not drunk at the time; not sleepy from drinking all night.

SOBRIETY, n. The solemn and austere dignity with which one observes another person who has just drunk a glass of strong drink.

SOCIAL NETWORKING, n. The use of an electronic device to connect friends and coworkers to one another regardless of their wishes, good judgment, or best interests.

SOCIALISM, n. 1. An ancient faith whereby men of good clothes, good means and good connections are permitted to live without working to support the less fortunate. 2. Briefly, the doctrine that all the ills of the world can be cured with a little more wealth for me, and a little less for everybody else. 3. The principle or system of society in which the means of production and distribution and exchange and the products are held in common, historically, by a predominance of self-employed laborers with access to productive property for subsistence and establishment. Uber for political ideologies. See also SIGNIFICANT SIDE-GIGGING. 4. The tenets and assertions of progressive Democrats, for which this dictionary can find no synonyms corresponding with external reality.

SOCIALIST, n. 1. One who desires that the laws of human society be more equitably adjusted than they are at present. 2. One who enjoys the labor of others equally with his own.

SOCIETY, n. 1. An organization of the whole human race for the prevention of cruelty to individual members of it. 2. In the present implementation of the Western world, a servitude of the many, for the pleasure and profit of the few. 3. The habits and manners of a particular class or type of individual, especially when contrasted to those of the same (or similar) type elsewhere. 4. A number of persons associated in one body for some common object. It is composed of three sorts: high rank; low rank, and those who see no rank. Those who believe themselves to be high are many, and those who believe themselves to be low are few. The most important, and rarest, type are those who see no rank.

SOJOURNERS, n. Travelers who stay at an inn. Rarely used by individuals to describe themselves.

SOLACE, n. The comfort a mourner gets from being sorry for someone who is dead.

SOLDIER, n. A person whose profession is murder and robbery but who is occasionally employed in other occupations.

SOLICIT, v. To ask for or try to obtain something from somebody who has it but will not give it.

SOLITUDE, n. 1. A state of mind produced by solitary confinement, or by the mere fact that one's friends are away. 2. The state of being forsaken by one's friends.

SON, n. A male human offspring; see INDIVIDUAL.

SONG, n. 1. A form of poetry the words of which are put together in a pleasing order, with nonsense in between. 2. Words set to music that are intended to be sung with the voice. Too often the only words in a singer's repertoire. Even worse are singers with Opinions. 3. A popular art consisting of words arranged to form an emotional but unintelligible internal rhyme, designed to be set to music and sung by a chorus of forty-seven trained sopranos and four army officers with vocal cords removed.

SORRY, adj. Feeling or showing grief; perturbed with sorrow.

SOUL, n. 1. A spiritual substance that animates a corporeal frame until the departure of the spirit. 2 The spiritual principle upon which we have bestowed our ignorance.

SOUTH, n. The part of America lying south of the Mason-Dixon line.

SPACE, n. The unknown environs beyond the earth's atmosphere. There, according to some reckoners, extends a comparatively vast region wherein human life is not impossible.

SPADE, n. A piece of dirt carried out to bury an animal alive.

SPEAK, v. To utter words that cannot be unheard.

SPECIAL GRAND JURY, n. A jury with a special power to find the accused not guilty without discussing the evidence or hearing the argument in support of either side.

SPENDTHRIFT, n. One who is content to consume this year the products of somebody else's labor, and promise for later a prudence he will never display unless he can persuade someone more charitable than himself to give him the same privilege next year.

SPIELBERG, STEVEN. n. Genius of animation and creator of Big Bang and dinosaurs for all generations.

SPIRITUAL, adj. The quality that distinguishes man from all other animals. It has no existence anywhere but in the human imagination.

SPIRITUALITY, n. 1. A morbid affection of the living for the dead. 2. A semi-occasional accompaniment of devout folk, chiefly remarkable for the lack of consistency of its manifestations. Its presence is manifested by unaccountable noises, strange lights, surprising energies, unusual psychic manifestations and unaccountable religious emotions. Its absence is entirely accounted for by natural laws.

SPONTANEOUS, adj. Immediately derived from an ignorant act or impulse; as, a spontaneous combustion.

SPOT, n. 1. A visible place without no corresponding image in the visual memory. (England) 2. A symptom of chronic ophthalmia appearing as dazzling points or small patches of occasional light before the retina.

SPYING, n. The obtaining of knowledge of the enemy's country by secret agents who are subject or who pretend to be subject to the enemy's laws, and who betray or pretend to betray the interests of their own country instead.

SQUARE, n. A quadrilateral figure with four equal sides and four right angles. It is part of the universal system devised for ensuring that nothing can be both attained and comprehended.

SQUID, n. A marine animal having ten long legs and arms too small to be of any use and two tapering tentacles furnished with strong suction discs for seizing and holding the prey. Obsolete; superseded by modern knowledge.

STAMMER, n. To speak with difficulty because of a partial impediment in the speech organs—such as a stick in the mouth. The stammerer's art consists in inducing heedless persons to pay for the unwholesome entertainment. Unkind.

STAN'S CAUGHT IN THE FOG, v. To let fly with a gun that previously missed its target, frequently aiming at a fellow soldier (if not accidentally killing him) on recommencing fire. This proverb was popularized in England in 1805 when the Royal Marine Stan Bunce killed Nelson at Trafalgar. Sadly mythical.

STANDARD, adj.1. Something set up as a measure or method of comparison. 2. Conforming to an established model or pattern; of established quality or make; not anomalous; ordinary of its kind; expected in a given situation. 3. Object of attachment, devotion or (perennially) hypothetical support.

STARS, n. 1. A certain kind of atmospheric speck that twinkles above such things as trees and waterfalls. 2. An invariable accompaniment of bad poetry. 3. Celestial bodies of hot gas whose radiations are often erroneously supposed to have something to do with the cooking of eggs.

STATE, n. Cockalorum governments in the United States.

STATISTICS, n. A branch of mathematics which consists in finding the averages that best satisfy you that the thing is true.

STAY, v.a. To cease to move; to stop; as, a ____stop, or a ____.

STEAM, n. The motive power of a locomotive expressed in pounds per square inch.

STEELE DOSSSIER, n. Humorous propositions repeated many times, especially in secret places, and intended to be believed.

STOCK MARKET, n. The only form of gambling in which the loser is guaranteed to know he has lost.

STORM, n. 1. Nature's declaration of war against mankind. 2. One of God's most unpleasant devices for reminding us that the world would not be what it is if He had made it Himself instead of buying so many cut-rate manufacturers of worlds from time to time.

STRANGER, n. One whom we meet by an appointment, but have not yet discovered his name. Death.

STRATEGY, n. In ancient warfare, the art of wearing out the enemy's troops without a pitched battle; in modern times, the art of war without combat; the non-combatant's occupation of killing time that he might live to kill again.

STREAM, n. A body of water pressing with force and rapidity against an unfortunate rock.

STRENGTH, n. possession of ample muscles on which to impose your will.

STRINGS, n. The things that make a harp or piano or other instrument sound.

STRUCTURE, n. The result of building. Order from Nothingness. "Look at these magnificent structures on magnetized paper!"

STUPID, adj. 1. Deficient in intelligence or mental power; lacking capacity for thought, reason, understanding, or reasonable judgment. 2. Affected with a defect in intellectual organ function not sufficient to qualify for an environmental covenant or onshore placement as hazardous waste, but typical of the majority of humans. 3. Incapable of appreciating the causes of things. Naturally deficient in intelligence. 4. Optimistic beyond all hope of rehabilitation. 5. Unreasonably annoyed at the stupid person who is annoying you. 6. Not a crime unless accompanied by malice aforethought.

SUBJECT, n. In the matter of rulers, an individual who yields a share in the sovereign power; in the matter of paintings and other artistic productions, a separate and indivisible part of that which composes.

SUBLIME, adj. In a bad way. In the opinion of Mr. W. H. Mallock, that eminent theologian: a sublime dilemma is one that cannot be solved both squarely and wisely; in other words, a dilemma that can be won only by one party and lost only by the other, and in respect to which all parties must admit themselves to be wrong before they can resolve it.

SUBVERSIVE, adj. 1. Disturbing to public peace and order because tending toward insurrection against lawful authority. 2. Tyrannical; not exercising official power according to law; seeking to overturn constituted society and set up a socialistic system in place thereof without duly recognizing or observing constitutional methods for doing so.

SUCCESS, n. 1. Achieved in despite of misfortune and misjudgment. 2. The one unpardonable sin against one's fellows. 3. In literature, the one unpardonable sin against oneself.

SUCCESSFUL, adj. Capable of competing successfully according to certain rules and conventions. In the American sense, meritorious.

SUFFER, v. 1. To be afflicted with an incurable source of pain, mental or physical. 2. To hold out for something yet to happen.

SUFFERING, n. One of the three unescapable afflictions of man. The other two are death and taxes.

SUICIDE, v. 1. The act or an instance of killing oneself intentionally. So called from the Latin *sui caedere*, to kill oneself. (Impressive that the AI knows this!) 2. An individual's folly; a family's destruction.

SUN, n. The center of the system whose invisible radiation makes it possible for us to exist on earth in a warm climate under an atmosphere protected from the solar radiation which otherwise would kill us. If that isn't confusing enough.

SUNDAY, n. 1. A day observed by certain peoples for the worship of a being they call "God." 2. A day set apart for distraction from the seriousness of the workweek. 3. A day set apart for the observance of one's own religion, or a day set apart for abstention from labor.

SUPREME BEING, n. The personage of the Christian Trinity to whom devotional attention is most urgently directed.

SURGEON, n. 1. A doctor skilled in cutting operative material from the body and so relieving spasms, congestions and other distresses. 2.A successful medical practitioner who commits great bodily harm on patients under the pretense of saving them.

SURPRISE, n. 1. The feeling of a person who before eating has been told that the dinner was supplied by a society to which he belongs. 2. A feeling of calm pleasure, lasting until something happens which should not have happened.

SURRENDER, v. To relinquish all hope of ever having a better time than the present.

SUSPICION, n. The feeling or idea we have when we do not know what it is that makes us feel suspicious.

SUSTENANCE, n. Something solid which is used to sustain a person until the next meal.

SWIPE, n. The act of thumbing one's nose at a fellow. A social error, much less grave than a poke in the eye with a sharp stick.

SYCOPHANT, n. A species of worm having no backbone—sometimes confounded with reptiles. Sycophant is here used as a term of disparagement — implying that the person so described would toad-eat whenever opportunity offered.

SYLLABLE, n. A unit of verse consisting of an unrhymed internal rhyme with all rhetoric functions fulfilled by its single foot or the final syllable thereof.

SYMPATHIZE, v. To have fellow-feeling with another's happiness, and to rejoice over his success without envying him.

SYMPATHY, n. 1. In modern use, a tender emotion excited by the trials or sufferings of another. 2. The virtue which induces us to share in the joys and sorrows of others. It is this virtue which divides men from brute beasts and gives us our highest title to be called human. 3. A special case of antipathy, in one who sees another suffering is able to disguise the natural joy that it is the Other who is suffering, rather than the Self.

SYMPHONY, n. A pleasing dish composed of slices of meat roasted and fried, various vegetables boiled and mashed together, French fried potatoes often appearing on the side, all served hot with gravy or tomato sauce.

TABOO, n. Anything forbidden by a particular law or custom.

TACO, n. A dish of Mexican origin consisting of a tortilla made of meal, fitfully fried.

TACTICS, n. Press agents' synonym for "strategy". As any student of military history knows, tactical genius is most often exhibited by generals who have just been defeated, or who wish to throw discredit on an allied commander.

TAG, n. The end, aim and object of the game called "tag," which is played with great zeal by boys.

TALK, n. The art of converting intermittent fits of silence into several days' mention of nothing in particular.

TAME, v.t. To reduce from a wild state, as by confining in captivity, subjecting to cultivation, or domesticating. Humans are hypothesized to be self-taming creatures.

TANTRUM, n. Temperamental disorder in children aged twenty-one years and over.

TARNISH, v. To reduce the metallic brightness of something by a dull layer of dirt obtained from public pavements or carriage wheels.

TAXES, n. The prices we pay for a civilized society. Stick with list prices, avoid fire sales.

TEA, n. 1. A fragrant beverage which induces refreshing sleep halfway through the day. 2. A substantial entertainment, quintessentially British, which compensates Christian travelers for the absence of a Starbucks.

TEACH, n. 1. One who makes another wiser than himself (usually for pay). 2. Convince oneself that he knows what he does not know.

TEACHER, n. 1. One who demonstrates the least knowledge and the greatest effort in a given domain. 2. One employed by an inconsequential school district to instruct pupils who will not be worth the trouble of teaching a few years hence. 3. One who makes others wise by his own example.

TEMPER, n. A sudden and ungovernable burst of anger.

TEMPERANCE, n. 1. A virtue whereby a man is rendered as harmless as those creatures which lack the power either to fight or fly. 2. A needless self-denial

TENDERFOOT, n. 1. The most conspicuous kind of adventure tourist—one who wears a cell phone collar. 2. A tourist who can't find his way home after having been turned around when facing the slightest obstacle, for instance, while following a country road that has no outlet.

TERRAIN, n. In military phraseology, the collective name for what isn't any damned use to an army unless it's on it—that is to say, "lucky earth."

TERRORISM, n. Unauthorized use of violence for political purposes.

TEXTBOOK, n. A book that is used in schools to teach children to read.

THANKFUL, adj. Feeling or showing gratitude; grateful. "Thankful for his morning cereal."

THANKSGIVING, n. 1. A day set aside by Americans of the past and of the present to express their immense gratitude either for a living pumpkin or for a dead turkey. 2. A festival commemorative of the murder of an entire people by another.

THAT, pron. & adverb. Indeed; truly; in truth. Frequently used with I as pronoun subject: I that am rudely terrible in my action, am the death of everyone who declares against me.

THEATRE, n. The art of representing human beings as beasts and monsters, either through the stage or the cinema. King Kong was great theatre.

THEME, n. The polite word for a lie which one wishes to pass off as unchallengeable truth.

THEOLOGY, n. 1. The science of the nature of the divine and its relations to humankind and to things. It is greatly concerned with things that nobody knows. 2. The science of how we got here; the cutting up of worn-out garments to reassemble the parts into the form of new garments and faith. 3. The dissection of God into the questions most easily answered. 4. The department of philosophy that deals with the relations between God and the creatures, specially man. There are only two divisions in this department-natural theology and revealed theology. The former consists in the study of God's works, and the latter—in attempting to understand God's revelation. Things might have been better arranged, but it would have been too easy. 5. The science of the nature of God and the limits of man's knowledge of Him. Between these limits : arguing.

THOUGHT, n. The intellectual process by which we think that we think.

TIARAS, n. The iron crowns once worn by sovereigns to denote their dignity and power; rarely worn in America where an enemy would have too great a chance of seizing it and throwing it back.

TIME, n. 1. A sort of medium whereby we measure the intervals between our experiences. 2. The continuum within which we happen to be immediately concerned; the thing that goes beyond all others in the ludicrousness of its acquisition.3. Season of stress and trouble; parent of worry, hurry, fear, and sorrow. 4. That which man is always trying to kill, but which ends in killing him. 5. That which man is certain of not having within his own control. 6. That which man is so eager to pass that he seldom enjoys, and so reluctant to enjoy that he seldom passes it well.

TIRE, v.t. To deprive a person of all interest in his surroundings.

TO THE HILT - to produce a distressing sensation between the shoulder blades.

TOGETHERNESS, n. 1. The quality of being in complete accord; as, to feel together. 2. Unable to tell which of two things goes first.

TOLERANCE, n. The virtue of a man who bears with the injuries that he himself inflicts.

TOMORROW, adv. In a certain sense, 'tomorrow' is right now.

TONGUE, n. An unruly member in man's mouth which plays the brute.

TONIGHT, n. A particular period of time between a day which ended last night and a day which begins tomorrow morning.

TOPIC, n. One's particular line of thought at a given time, chosen mostly because he was reminded of it by an adjacent factor.

TOURISM, n. An ingenious device invented by the compilers of dictionaries to explain how they came to illustrate with pictures the words they cannot otherwise define.

TOURIST, n. A traveler who carries his own hotel upon his back.

TOWNSHIP, n. An incorporated village. Its principal industry is a man who makes coffins.

TRADE, n. One of the many methods by which fools become rich and wise people poor.

TRAIN, n. A railroad for conveying coal from the mine to the seaport. With such an arrangement Ireland could soon be civilized.

TRAVEL, n. 1. The art of traveling, or going from place to place, with a horse, or other beast of burden. 2. The art or act of moving from one point to another; the means thereto, whether by walking or riding. 3. The only means of seeing the world.

TRAVELER n. an unlucky person journeying from one place to another by coach or train on land: one who is obliged to find any passage for himself and has not the assistance of a travel agent at either end of his journey

TREASURE, n. A thing that confers a crazy pleasure, clogging rational enjoyment and expression with an ecstasy whose object is outside life.

TREASURE, n. In the context of "seeking treasure," an unprofitable occupation, unless you are Nicolas Cage.

TREMORS, n. Consecutive shivers in the wake of an earthquake.

TRIUMPH, n. 1. The plural form of GENERAL. 2. Viewing with self-approval the discomfiture and capitulation of an enemy, or a friend. 3. Something obtained by an armed occupation which creates a feeling of unjustified moral superiority.

TRUE LOVE, n. A love needing neither pledge nor fulfillment.

TRUE, adj. 1. Consistent with reality, or with itself. 2. The opposite of false. 3. According to the tenets of some sect or other a distinction which has reference to nothing outside itself.

TRUMP, IVANKA. 1. The daughter of an American President and his favorite child. 2. A person who is a cross between a trout and a flounder.

TRUST, v. To give one's confidence in return for moral or legal security.

TRUTH n. 1. The principle or quality of being in accord with fact or reality; accuracy, verity. 2. A class of concepts having the quality of being apparently incontroverted all unprovable. 3. plausible succession of words calculated to mislead while conveying an impression that they tend to establish truth. 4. A statement universally acknowledged to be true because nobody believes it. 5. A successful lie told with due regard to the nature of the audience. 6. An ingenious compound of desirability and appearance. 7. The daughter of time.

TRUTHFUL, adj. 1.Affirmative of that which is; a word if used freely, so discordant in its significations that it offends the ears of truth. 2. Unskilful in the invention of falsehoods. 3

TURKEY, n. 1. A large farm bird, known to naturalists as Meleagris Americana, noted for its excellent qualifications for drawing out gravy. A great demand exists for the flesh of young turkeys; it is a favorite dish on festive occasions. Older turkeys are not so easily obtained and therefore they go off at a great advantage to dealers in secondhand poultry products. 2. A large bird whose flesh when eaten on certain religious anniversaries has the peculiar property of attesting piety and gratitude.

TWEET, n. The wrath of the Devil.

TYRANT, n. A person who holds absolute authority over a city.

U

UGLY, adj. Incomprehensible to the general public.

UNCONSCIOUS, adj. Unable to trouble themselves to talk.

UNDERSHIRT, n. A shirt worn under one's clothes in order to keep the latter clean. Protection against cold is an ancillary benefit.

UNITY, n. The quality or state of being one, indivisible, inconceivable of separation.

UNIVERSE, n. 1. An imaginary unity to which we owe allegiance, allegiance being of the same origin as belief and disbelief, only even more enigmatic. 2. The cosmic affair in which we seem to nominally exist.

UP-TO-DATE, adj. Wholly ignorant of what has taken place since one's last screen refresh.

USEFULNESS, n.: The social activity most needed and least wanted.

UTILITARIAN, n. One who makes the happiness of a single person his chief endeavor.

VAGRANCY, n. a Christian pilgrimage.

VAGUENESS, n. The degree by which the meaning of a word is blurred or uncertain.

VALENTINE, n. The day celebrating the love whereof chalky white heart emblems are given in token; the kind of love which is a fatuous opposition to hate, and valuable chiefly as an influence to engender the economically valuable process of mutual infatuation.

VALOR, n. The animal courage that makes a Marie Antoinette say "Let them eat cake," or a young American pastor's son say "Let him who is without sin cast the first stone."

VALUE, n. That which, in the estimate of others, has no value; that inestimable quality which renders an article good, bad or indifferent.

VAMPIRES, n. Ghouls that generally appear in human form during the day but by night have acquired or take the form of bats, rats, owls, cats, or wolves. They haunt various solitary places and suck the blood of men or cattle.

VENGEANCE, n. 1. An instrument of divine justice. 2. The act of inflicting punishment for crime without doing anything to improve the criminal's disposition.

VERB, n. The only part of speech in English that can act as a subject, a predicate, or an object.

VERNACULAR, n. The language spoken by a particular group or class of persons; the patois used by a certain social stratum; the speech used by a country as distinguished from that which is proper to another country or to other countries in general. It is more especially (1) the popular language employed during a temporary illness; (2) the habitual speech of one's place, role, or epoch; (3) language peculiar to certain subcultures in England: Polari.

VEST, n. A garment which covers the upper part of one's body, commonly used as the polite covering of the surface of the true grief that is under it.

VETERAN, n. A person who has served his country in war so well that he can no longer be persuaded to give out the facts about it.

VICE, n. A social evil whose presence nobody seriously denies and whose departure no one seriously desires.

VICTORY, n. The act of defeating an enemy or opponents; the overthrow of an opponent in a struggle; a success resulting from such a conflict; the accomplishment of an object sought after by effort; cause for rejoicing or triumph.

VIRGIN, n. A woman without peer.

VIVE LA DIFFERENCE! Hello globally inclusive speech and good-bye and good riddance to the tiresome, interfering, jejune, ridiculous, American monoculture. Vive la difference!

VOLUME, n. A kind of surface constructed synthetically for large human individuals to lie upon when a chair or bed is inadequate. BEAN BAG; PIER.

VOTE, n. A prayer for good governance recorded in numbers and efficacy verified by scratching the head.

WALL, n. A structurally unsound expedient adopted during pharaonic Egypt to prevent the ingress of sand.

WALLET, n. A device containing a modern polygonal representation of money.

WAR, n. 1. A by-product of the arts of peace. 2. A by-product of human nature whose sweep can be bounded only by its duration. 3. A service provided when all other services fail to deliver enough revenue to keep a government afloat. 4. A thing that kings, emperors and congresses of nations find useful. 5.A source of patriotic songs and happy thoughts on the part of the patriotic; a disagreement from which great prosperity for the hopeful patriots is to emerge.

WAR, n. On the part of military forces, an unathletic contest with guns and bayonets by which they seek to prevent the carnage that would result from rushing directly into combative contact with an enemy.

WARD, n. 1. One who is put into a jail or kept in confinement under legal arrest; a prisoner. 2. One who is placed in custody of an executor, trustee or other court officer whose business it is to take charge of the affairs of another until a will can be probated or administration granted; an interim guardian. 3. An assistant to a caped crime fighter.

WARMTH, n. The state in which we inspire

WASTE, n. The natural result of converting wealth into waste-paper. A thing denied by the gods.

WATCH, n. A device intended to measure and indicate the hours and minutes during which its owner does not wear it.

WAY, n. The highway a man travels in his mind, on which there are an endless number of "signs" stopping the traveler at every turn. And just as he begins to think he is clear of them and rejoices in having got past, he sees the most fatal one of all — STOP!

WEAKNESS, n. The willingness of a writer to subjugate structural integrity to the considerations or whims of persons or organizations paying for the structure.

WEALTH, n. Any blessing that money can buy.

WEDDING, n. The ceremonial sealing-off of a woman's right hand.

WEREWOLF, n. A wolf that resembles a man.

WHAT, interrogative pronoun. The word interrogatively applicable to all nouns, pronouns, adjectives, verbs and adverbs.

WIDOWER, n. One who mourns the loss of a wife, not having had the foresight to insure his estate against her loss.

WIFE, n. A woman with whom a man cohabits; by extension on the Western Island, all the women on her side of the family. "I'll take it up with my wife" denotes an interminable series of discussions among matriarch of every age and rank.

WILD, adj. Inhabiting an uncultivated tract; not under control of man. Often used as epithet expressing aversion or distaste.

WIND, n. 1. An anthem of praise whispered in honour of some very private and secret person. Rare. 2. A symphony commemorating some digestive event best conducted in private.

WINE, n. Fermented grape juice known as "grapes."

WISDOM, n. 1. The part of knowledge that consists in the recognition of ignorance and error. 2. Knowledge of how little can be known. 3. Acquired and contented stupidity.

WISHINGWELL, n. A reverse wishing fountain which squirts water at the visitor, then demands payment.

WITLESS, adj. 1. Devoid of intelligence. 2. Relating to the intellectual faculties in general or some of them; but not to any particular one; as to a person whose head or heart lacks intelligence or feeling respectively.

WITTY, adj. Extremely clever and original; aggressively staving off the forces of entropy; too smart for this world.

WOKEISM, n. 1. a religion that is popular with what can be described as "woke" people. 2. Worship of or by social justice warriors.

WOMAN, n. 1. An animal usually living in the outskirts of civilization, which dresses according to the fashion, subsists mostly on high-fiber food and tranquilizers, and bears each year but one offspring or none at all. 2. A person with a striking body who is believed to be endowed with great sexual power and a deep desire for too much: those who cannot afford the high fees of courtesans often indulge themselves with the imagination of one woman, while those wealthy enough to buy a sexual slave often avoid such fantasies because they are identical with fact. Obsolete. 3. An animal usually living in the vicinity of Man, and having a tail adapted to his use, but inconvenient to hers; as, a horse. Vulgar. 4. An animal usually living in the neighborhood of Man, and having a rudimentary susceptibility to domestication. It is credited by popular opinion with special beauty, artfulness, and predisposition to certain human uses.

WOMEN and MARRIAGE, n. The twin sisters who are for ever struggling to wreak the ills of man and human life; man's most inveterate foe and natural predator. Obsolete and, if anything, the reverse of the truth.

WORK, n. 1. The labor which a person does in order to live. 2. The kind of exertion which, properly speaking, produces nothing, but which is good for the character for those who are not engaged in the occupation. 3. The kind of tedious effort that was originally imposed as a punishment upon the condemned and is now largely inflicted upon those who are not deservedly punished.

WORLD, n. 1. The sphere over which its human inhabitants exert a dominion that is both comprehensive and strictly unnecessary. 2. The imaginary sphere invented by English and other northern philosophers as a gibe at the unphilosophic simplicity of their southern neighbors. See FIRST WORLD. 3. A level surface, somewhat larger than the state of Indiana, to which American exports its rural labor surplus in the form of global military deployment.

WORRIED, adj. 1. Perplexed or anxious about some remote event; not disposed to take trouble for the present; wanting confidence. 2. Having the mind upset by the contemplation of one's bread and butter. 3. Consumed by a fear of something that does not, as yet, exist.

WORRY, n. 1. A species of melancholy closely allied to megrim. Its characteristics are insularity, long-windedness, and inability to defend oneself simultaneously against little and great evils. 2. To show that one is giving way to misgiving, which is the beginning of wisdom. 3. The work of a fool at some time not specified. 4. Purchasing one's freedom from the troubles which the Law of Causality has laid on us.

WORSHIP, v. To venerate expectantly, or to honour with ceremony due to a divine being.

WORTH, n. 1. Qualitative distinction between one thing and another; that quality which sets diamond apart from coal. 2. A word formerly much used in connection with donations to the deserving poor, now commonly used in connection with what remains after the unworthy have taken all they want. 3. That quality of a person's character that inspires respect, admiration and love. The word is from an Old English word meaning "worthiness."

WORTHY, adj. Mistakenly thought by the speaker to have qualities that transcend the norm of human unimportance.

WRITING, n. The art of improving on GPT-3 output by adding new things and removing old ones.

YAWN, n. The act of opening one's mouth wide and inhaling mightily. It operates to relieve subsequently the natural exhaustion of having done so.

YESTERDAY, adj. The first day of time immemorial.

YOUNG, adj. Inexperienced in wickedness, as a virgin just marooned ashore relative to a Hell-directed Pyrate.

YOUR, adj. Belonging to some one else, at least temporarily, and in theory.

Z

ZENITH, n. The point of the heavens directly above the observer or the place where a star or planet appears on the meridian every night.

ZIP, n. A sudden start; a swift, decisive movement.

ZIPPER, n. A mechanical device for arresting the progress of dresses and trousers which embrace all subjacent surfaces.

ZOO, n. A prison in which animals go when they are not wanted at home.

[0-9]

2020, n. The year that will end this miserable experiment in human self-government and usher in a mercifully brief era of tyranny. Obsolete, and, fortunately, untrue.

ABOUT THE PUBLISHER

Fred Zimmerman is the Publisher of Nimble Books LLC, an innovative, idiosyncratic independent publishing house with more than 400 editions in print. Authors are welcome to submit manuscripts created entirely or in part by OpenAI's GPT-3 or other algorithmic publishing tools. To learn more, go to www.NimbleBooks.com.